This book belongs to

MY HOME

Window
Balcony
Trees
Stairs
Street Light
Plants
Name-Plate
Road
Pavement

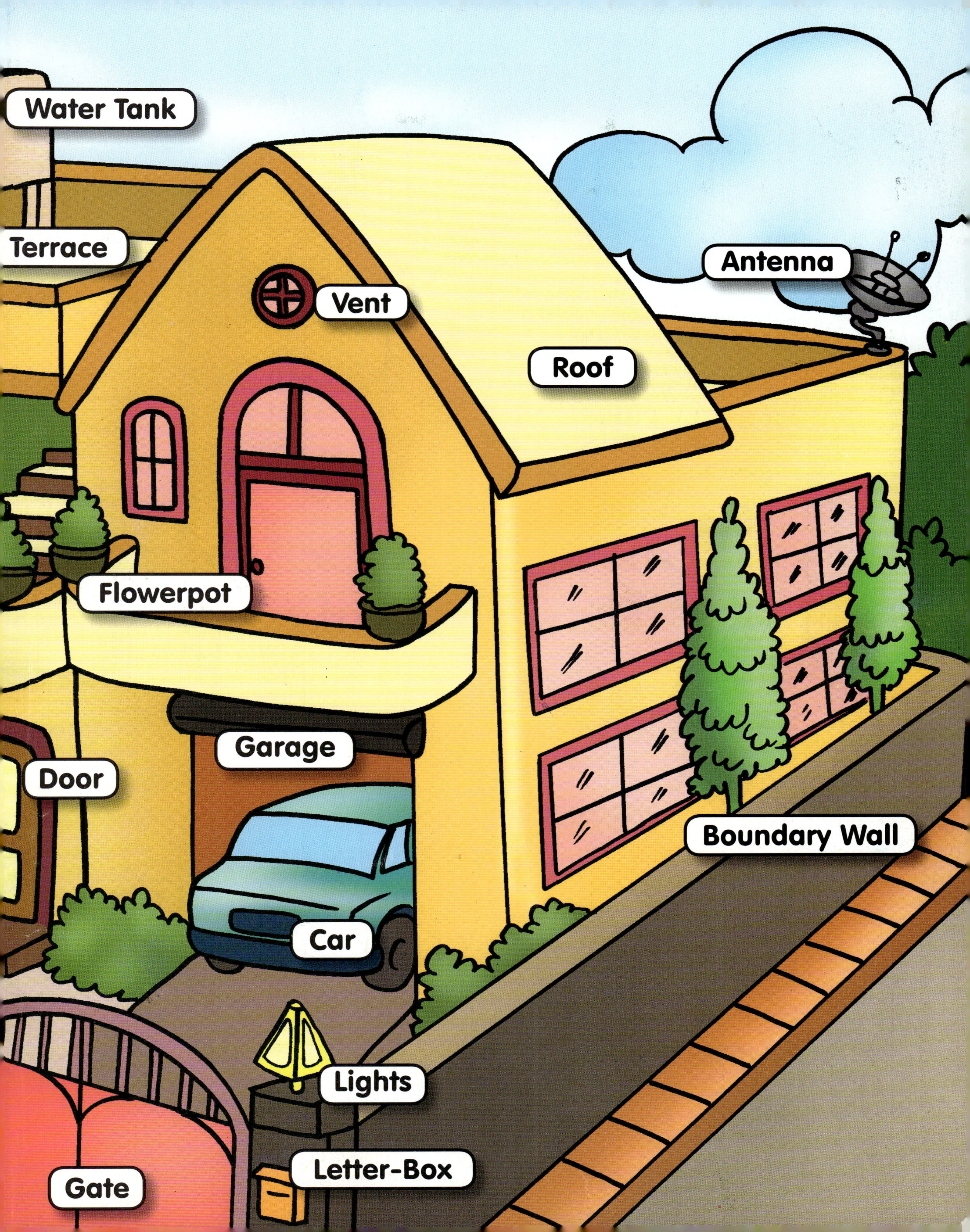

Water Tank
Terrace
Vent
Roof
Antenna
Flowerpot
Garage
Door
Boundary Wall
Car
Lights
Letter-Box
Gate

Curtain
Television
Window
Flowerpot
Remote Control
Pet
Sofa
Table
TIMES
Newspaper
Telephone

Books
Toy
Music System
Cabinet
Carpet
Fruits
Lamp
Cellular Phone
LIVING ROOM

DINING ROOM

Window
Wash-basin
Cabinet
Chair
Table-Mat
Rice
Floor
Glass
Pet
Water Jug

Tray
Door
Refrigerator
Fruits
Plate
Bowl
Knife
Fork
Dining Table

MY ROOM
Rack
Books
Curtain
Shirt
Chair
Table Lamp
Diary
Table
Pen stand
Pen

Wall Clock
Painting
Poster
Photo Frame
Toy
Pillow
Lamp
Bed Sheet
Side Table
Ball
Mat
Aeroplane

Window
Serving Spoons
Jar
Cooking Utensils
Pressure Cooker
Gas Stove
Vegetables
Gas Cylinder
Dustbin
OUR KITCHEN

Cabinet
Towel
Toaster
Kettle
Bread
Oven
Wash-basin
Milk Bottle
Mixer/Juicer
Refrigerator

Shower
Cabinet
Mirror
Soap
Shampoo
Tap
Foam
Toy
Bath-Tub

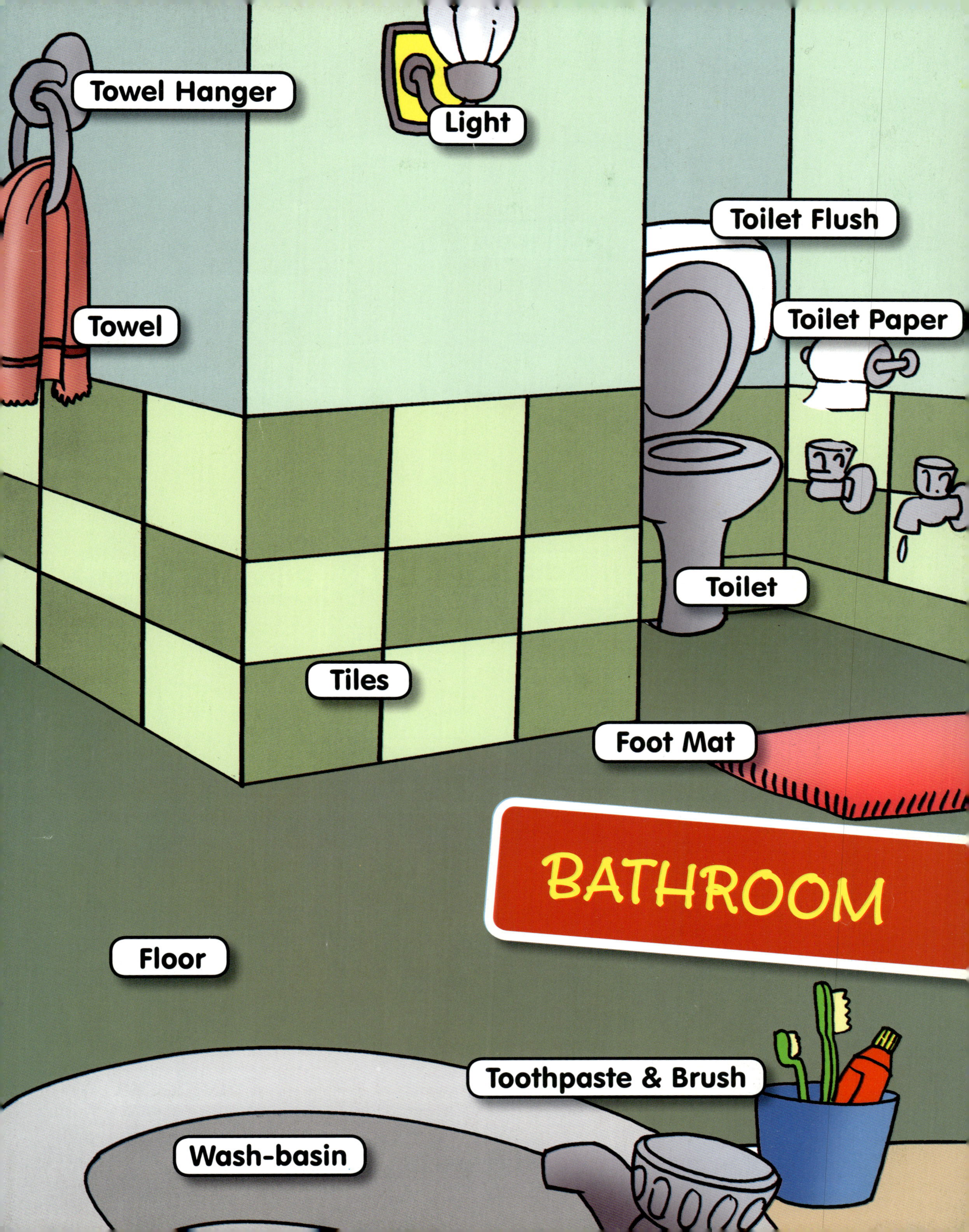
Towel Hanger
Light
Toilet Flush
Towel
Toilet Paper
Toilet
Tiles
Foot Mat
BATHROOM
Floor
Toothpaste & Brush
Wash-basin

St. Merry's
Window
Door
Classroom
School Building
Principal's Room
Bushes
Tree
Plants
Light
MY SCHOOL
Boundary Wall

chool
Clouds
Activity Room
School Bus
SCHOOL BUS
Stairs
Teacher
School Bag
Gate
Pavement
Student

Chart
Notice-Board
Blackboard
Wall
Teacher
Chalk
Duster
MY CLASSROOM
Table
Pencil
Eraser
Dustbin

Window
Poster
Door
Books
Student
Pen
Desk
Bench

Gardener
School Building
Plants
Slide
Watering Pipe
Shuttlecock
Girl
Racket
Grass
See-Saw
Boy
Flower

Ball
Tree
Bush
USE ME
Dustbin
Swing
PLAYGROUND

AUDITORIUM
Balcony
Exit Sign
EXIT
Microphone
Audience
Seat
Chief Guest
Stage Light
Speaker

KIT
Exit Gate
Cameraman
Curtain
Spot Light
Camera
Actor
Stage

Footwear Shops
KG GARMENTS
SALE
Garment Shop
Restaurant
OFF
50%
Mannequins
Security Guard
Escalator
Ice-Cream Parlour
Display Board
SHOPPING MALL

Shops
Cosmetics Shop
M. JEWELLERS
Jewelry Shop
Food Court
Mini Rides
Popcorn
Shopping Bag

CINEMA HALL

Fire Extinguisher
EXIT
Movie
Curtains
Speakers
Seat
D5
D4
D3
Seat Number
D2
Floor

Roof Lights
Projector
Projector Room
Balcony
EXIT
Exit Door
Ticket
Audience
Cold Drink
Popcorn

Wall
Zebra
Ducks
Elephant
ZOO
Guard
Cage
Tiger
Meat
Bear

Giraffe
Monkey
Lion
Safety Fence
Visitors
Dustbin

HOSPITAL
Drip
Stand
Injection
Partition
Pillow
Stethoscope
White Coat
Doctor
Patient
Bed Sheet
Medicines

Ambulance
Stretcher
Ward Boy
Bed
Nurse
Dustbin
Bandage
Wheelchair

RAILWAY STATION
Window
Door
Coach
Platform
Benches
Food Stall
Passenger
Trolley
Luggage
Escalator

Clock
Shed
Train
Engine
Track
Ticket Inspector
Book Stall
Travel Bag
Goods

Building
Fence
Driver
Rearview mirror
Route number
912
Windscreen
Door
Spectacles
Bus
Coat
Road
Bus number
Bumper
MR.VL92
Car
Tyre
Zebra crossing
Trousers
AT BUS STOP

Bus routes
234 912
778
937
Bus stop
Seats
Ticket
Step
Bag
Shirt
Passengers
Briefcase
Footpath

Window
Curtain
Wall painting
Waiter
Bow
Table
Glass
Bowl
Tray
Flower vase
Menu
Chair
Table cover
Headphones
Food
Ice-cream
RESTAURANT

Wall
Lamp
Door
Customer
Pen
Telephone
Doormat
Reception
Fish

WATER PARK
Tree
Bushes
Canopy
Speaker
Shower
Glasses
Swimming trunks
Children
Tube

Slide
Spiral slide
Ball
S-slide
Platform
Water
Splash
Swimsuit
Straw
Soft drink
Towel

Ribbons
Birthday cap
Moustache
Father
Collar
Knife
Hair band
Soft-drink
Birthday presents
BIRTHDAY PARTY

Balloons
Banner
DAY
Birthday boy
Mother
Candle
Icing
Cake
Ponytail
Sweets
Table
Skirt
Table cloth

AT THE PICNIC

Rainbow
Balloons
Fishing rod
Hat
Waterfall
Feather
Bush
Chair
Fishing
Family
Fish
Bucket
Pier
Spectacle
River
Picnic hamper
Mat

AT THE BEACH

Coconut
Leaves
Tree
Sea
Surfer
Player
Surf-board
Conch
Footprints
Sand

Beach ball
Sky
Sun
Umbrella
Tube
Net
Drink
Beach chair
Shovel
Flag
Sea Shell
Pail
Sandcastle
Bucket

Merry-go-round
Hat
Roller-coaster
Tent
Ice-cream stall
Magic show
Vendor
Cap
Ice-candy
T-shirt
Toy-stall
Pocket
Teddy bear
Visitors
AT THE FAIR

Ferris-wheel
Balloons
Joker
Movie Show
Ticket clerk
Ticket
Ticket counter
Queue

Tree
Scare Crow
Hat
Feather
Fence
Beard
Duck
Duckling
Farmer
Pond
Shovel
Stone
Coop
Grass
Cock
Hen
Comb
Pocket
Fodder
FARM